This Turtle Coloring Book Belongs To

Turtles
Coloring Book for Kids

Kids who like turtles must have one

This incredible Kids coloring book
for Turtles lovers.

It has over **40** had-paintes pitures of turtles to make your mind feel pleasures.

Coloring all these pitures will help someone to get free of stress and this coloring book will be useful to enjoy the time.

Now get your Reptiles animal kids coloring book!

Kids who like turtles must have one!

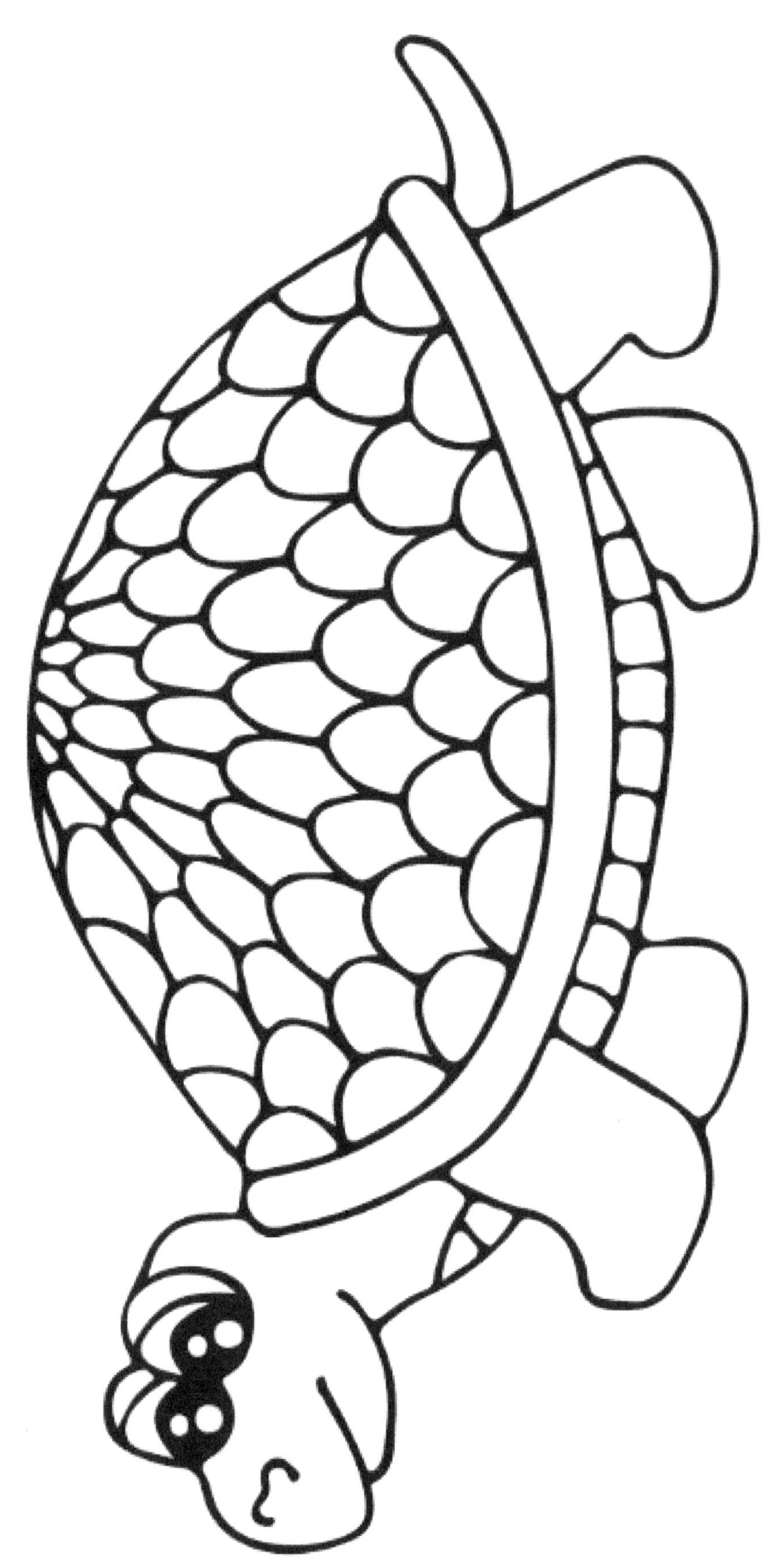

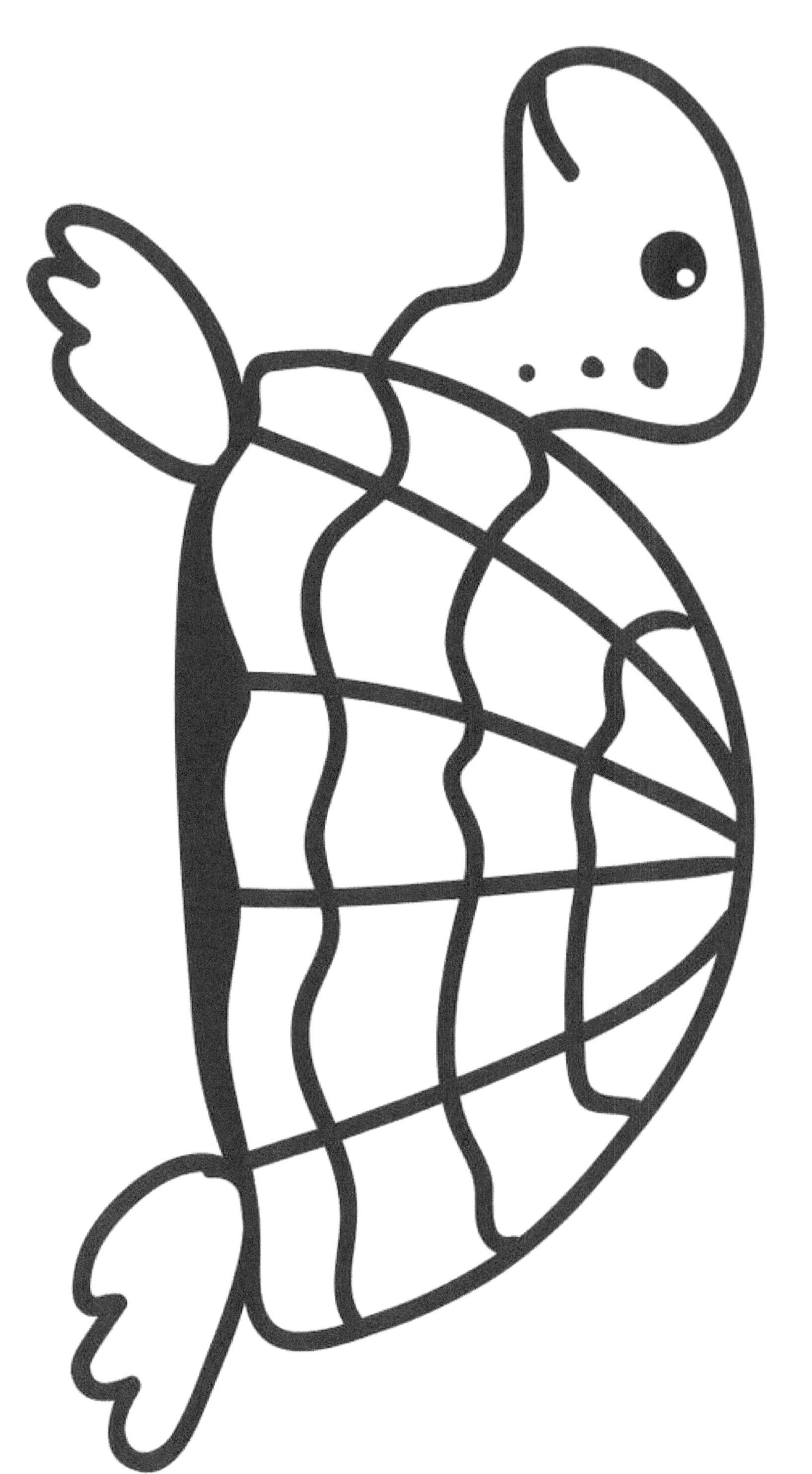

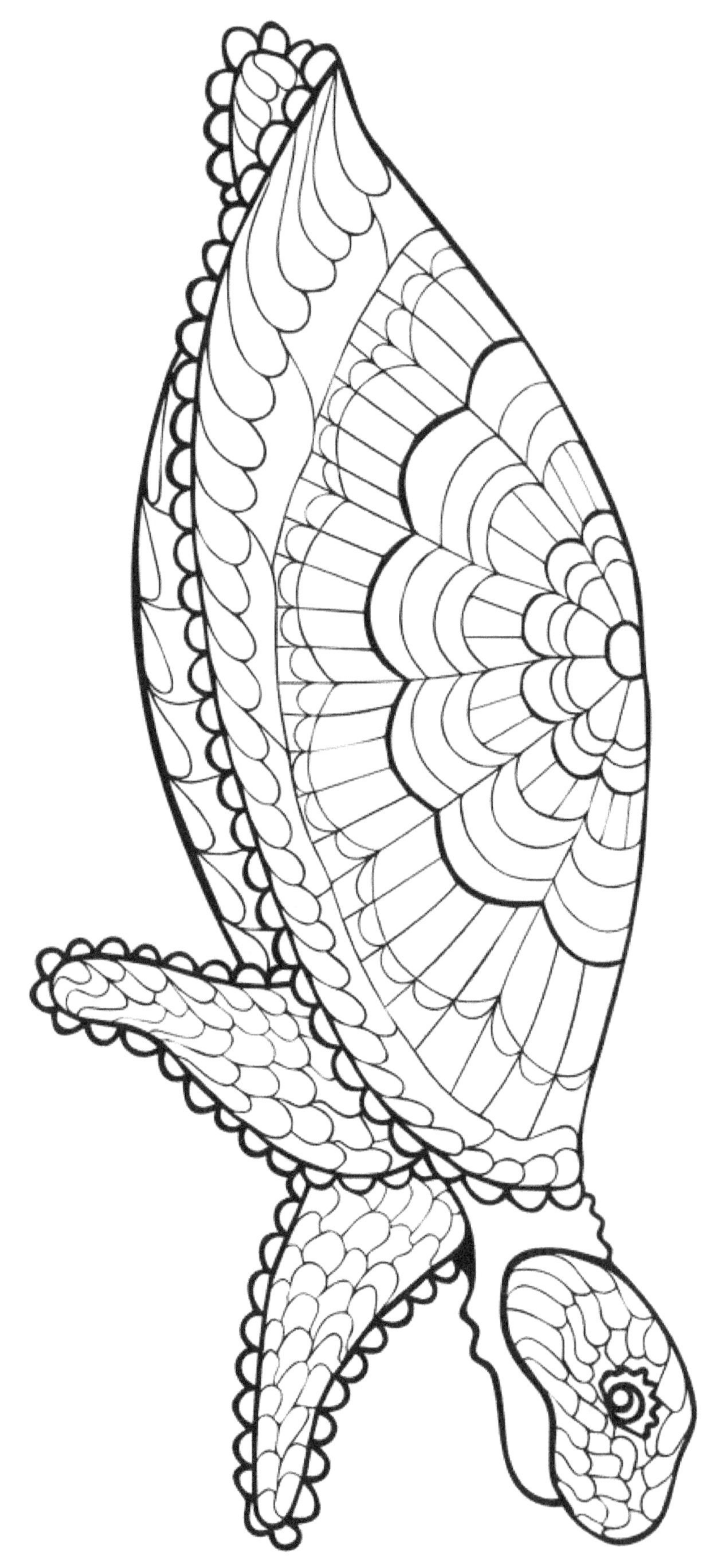

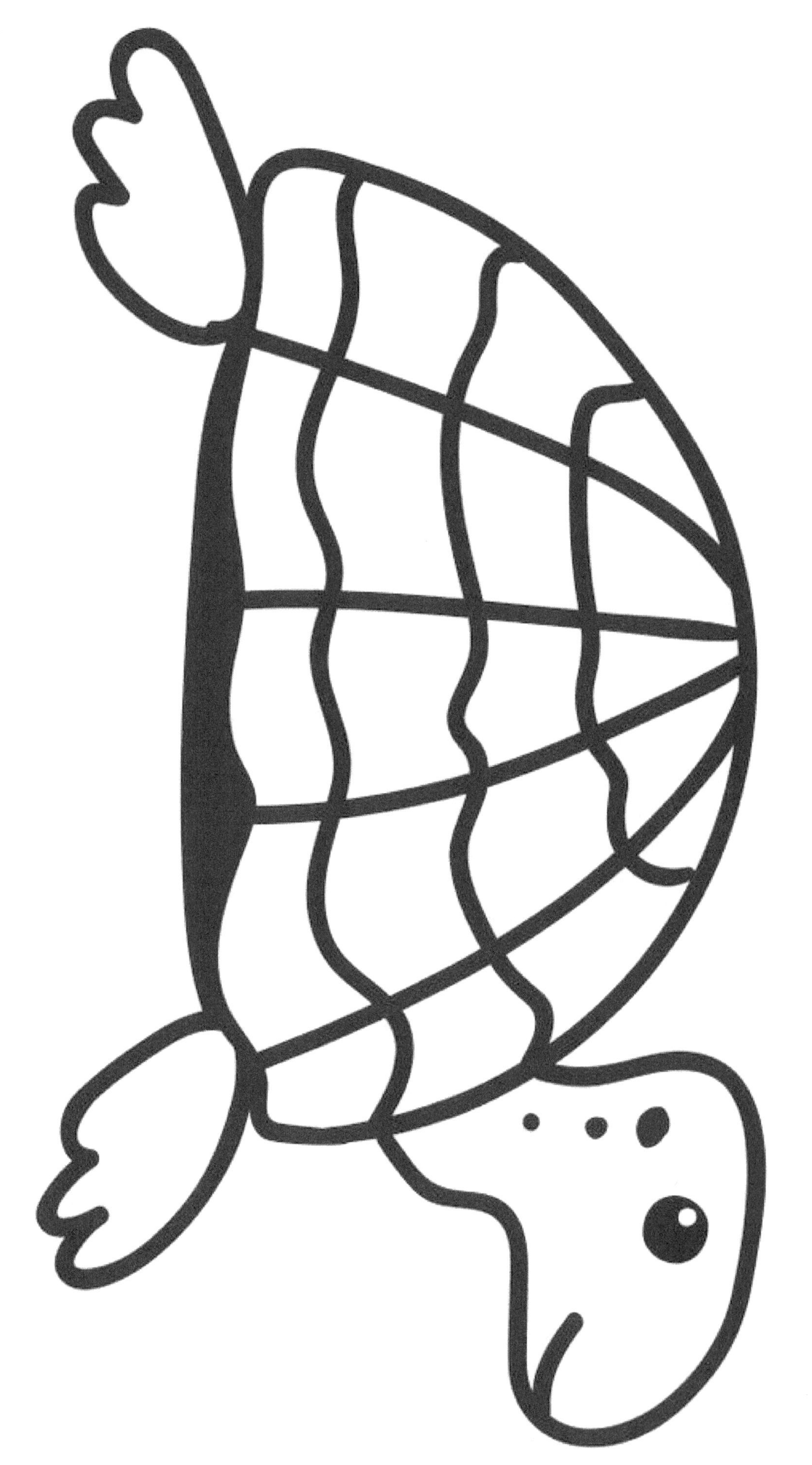

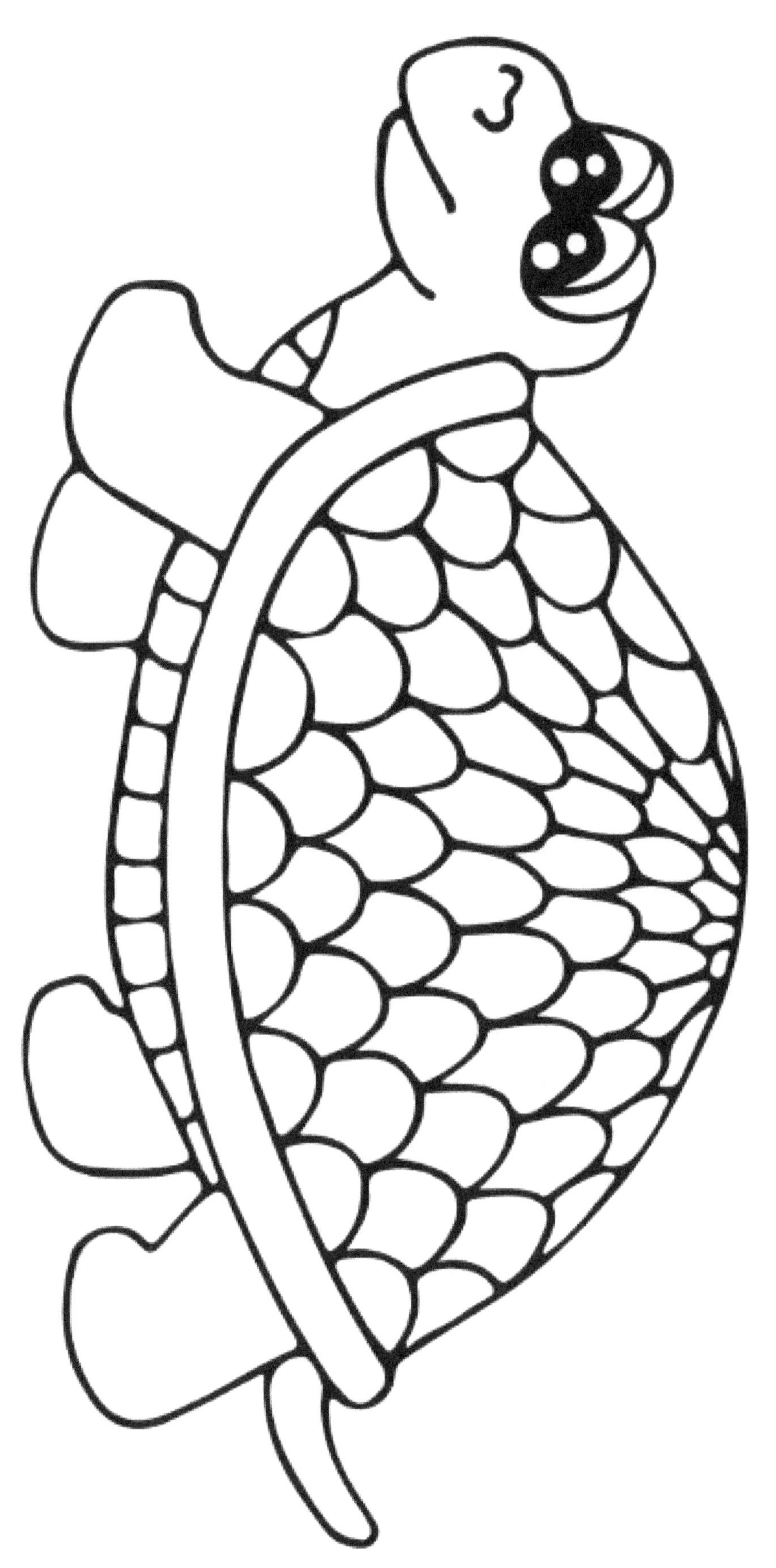

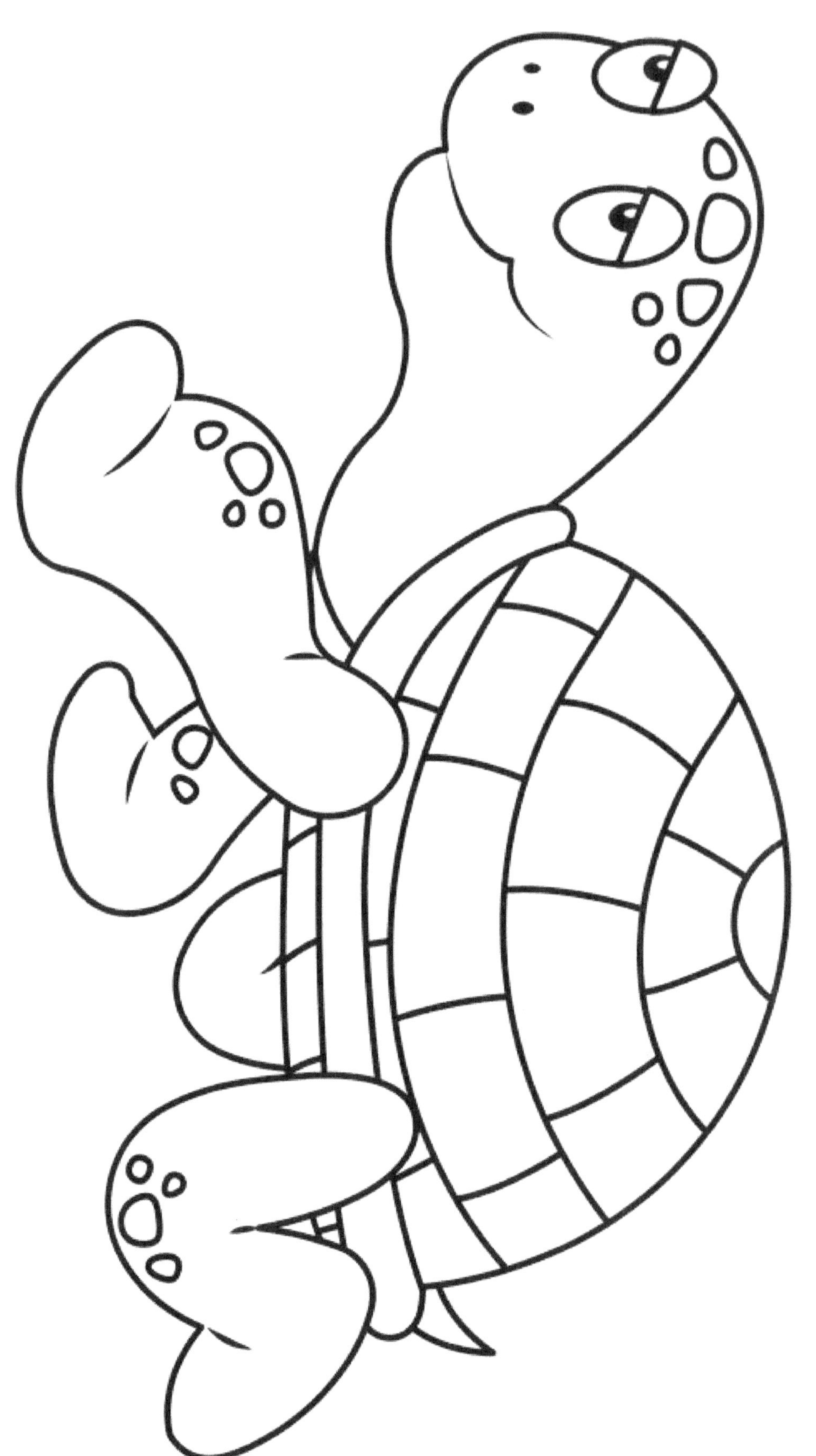